Your Own Quiet Time

Presented to

Quiet time

Let mee sleep

New Revised Edition

MERIDIAN
SLIMLINES

A Christian Classic
New Revised Edition

This edition is published by special arrangement with and permission of InterVarsity Press.

Published in 1991 by Meridian, Grand Rapids, MI 49546

Reissued 1995 by Meridian, Grand Rapids, MI.

M0104 Paperback Gift Edition
ISBN 1-56570-010-4

Book design: Gayle Raymer and
Cover design: David M. Versluis

Manufactured in the
United States of America

INTRODUCTION

If authority were needed for observing an early morning Quiet Time, the writings and example of men of God in all ages would supply it. But the practice of our Master himself, who, "rising up a great while before day, went out, and departed into a solitary place, and there prayed," is sufficient evidence of its supreme importance for us.

If he who was never out of touch with his Father could not dispense with definite and prolonged seasons of retirement for fellowship with him, how much less can we?

Read the story of his crowded day in Mark 1:21-34. Notice how, in spite of the great pressure of work, he was up long before dawn to seek his Father's face—and then ask yourself whether your excuses for omitting a Quiet Time can ever be valid.

But it is one thing to be convinced of the necessity of forming this habit, and quite another to observe it with persevering regularity. Moreover, it is not sufficient to have the time at one's disposal, for the half-hour—more or less—which you set aside for your

Quiet Time may easily be frittered away, almost wasted.

In what follows we wish not only to emphasize the necessity of spending time alone with God, but to give valuable, practical suggestions about *how* the time may be spent to the best advantage.

FELLOWSHIP WITH GOD

That God desires our fellowship is, perhaps, one of the most amazing facts conveyed to us through the Scriptures.

This fact is so staggering in its conception that it is extremely difficult for us fully to grasp and consider its significance.

That God should allow his creatures to have fellowship with himself is wonderful enough; but that he can *desire* it, that it gives him satisfaction and joy and pleasure, is almost too much for understanding!

"The Father *seeks* such to worship him ..." Let this reflection fasten itself upon us, and it will inspire us with a passionate desire to seek his face morning by morning. The usual conception—that we read our Bibles and say our prayers for our own benefit and satisfaction—will fade into insignificance. Let this simple thought of his desire for our fellowship obsess us morning by morning and day by day.

It will carry us through times of deadness

and darkness, give us patience to continue and persevere, when we remember that he is waiting to be gracious to us, waiting till he sees that we wait upon him.

WHY GOD CAN LET US TALK WITH HIM

It is deeply important that the cross of our Lord Jesus Christ be given its proper place. There can be no fellowship with God on any other basis. I know this sounds commonplace enough. You will remember that in the Old Testament, God ordained that the sacrifice should be offered daily, morning by morning.

Does not this speak to us? With us, too, morning by morning there should be a definite, conscious, prayerful, praiseful *realization* of the blessed sacrifice of God's Son. It is at the Mercy Seat that God has promised to meet us. One of the saints of the last century wrote, "Never have I felt a greater need of the blood of Christ than I do today, and never have I been enabled to make such use of it." Can we say this as we draw near to a holy God?

And here I may add a warning: Let us beware lest, if we do not immediately derive any subjective satisfaction or conscious appreciation from this exercise, we conclude that it is of no avail. God is seeking for men and women who will worship. Let us then worship, whether we derive any conscious benefit from it or not. Christ is worthy to be praised!

As we set ourselves to worship and praise him for his wondrous sacrifice, seeking to *give* rather than get, we shall find that the Holy Spirit will silently, but very really, convey to us the efficacy of his death and make our fellowship with God through the Word and prayer a blessing and delight. Let us believe that Christ and his atoning death are worthy of everlasting praise and adoration, whether we actually derive any conscious benefit or not. Let us keep our eyes off ourselves and our own subjective experience, and keep them fixed by faith in worship and wonder on the Lord Jesus and him crucified. God will see to it that we are blessed thereby, for "them that honor me," he has said, "I will honor."

AN AFFECTIONATE CONFIDENCE IN GOD

In all our reading of his Word and in all our praying our greatest need is a warm and living and expectant faith, what Charles Finney called an "affectionate confidence" in God. "Without this it is impossible to please him." The one object of our devotions should be to eliminate everything that will keep us from believing God utterly. "This is the work of God," said Christ, "that you believe ..." "All things are possible to him who believes."

In the seventeenth chapter of St. Luke's Gospel, faith is likened to a seed. If the seed we planted in our garden a week ago could speak to us, it would tell us how cold and dark and damp and hard was its environment. We would reply in the language of St. Peter, "After you have suffered a little while, the God of all grace will make you perfect; establish, strengthen, settle you." This is the story of a living faith planted in our hearts by the Holy Spirit. When patience has done its perfect work, our faith will turn to sight.

In all our Bible reading, therefore, and in all our praying during the Quiet Hour, do let us see that before we leave the room, faith has brought us into this quiet resting place—of wonder that God desires our fellowship, of worship at the place called Calvary, and of working throughout the day the "work of God," even an affectionate confidence in his dear Son.

USE OF THE BIBLE IN THE QUIET TIME

I have been asked to say something about how to use the Bible for maximum profit in the Quiet Time, and I will do so in a way as simple and practical as possible, drawing from my own experience.

MAKE TIME

The first and obvious thing to say is that *there must be* a Quiet Time.

No one can say for another what time in every twenty-four hours is the best, because our circumstances and duties are so infinitely varied. But, if the proposed benefit is to be ours, we must have a time. Some will find early morning most convenient, others late night, and others again have time at their disposal during the day; but, whenever it may be, the time should be fixed.

It is strange and sad that we organize pretty well everything except our religious life. We organize our study, our meals, our recreation, our sleep—but we leave the needs of our souls to take care of themselves as and when they can.

No one who organizes three meals a day for his body can say that he cannot possibly fix a time daily for Bible meditation. Such an affirmation is a loud advertisement of spiritual indifference. A sense of absolute need will soon become creative.

Some are able to give more time and some less, but *all*, if they are to live, must give *some* time. That time should be *fixed*. It should be as regular a part of the daily program as the morning wash or the evening meal. *Before you read any further, do something about deciding on a time.*

FIND A QUIET PLACE

Second, *there should be a quiet place.*

I know that this may present a problem. At home there may be a large family, at school you may have a roommate. It may be difficult to get away alone at a given hour each day, but the effort should be made. If entire aloneness is impossible, then the next best thing must be done. But a certain value drops out of the Quiet Time when there is no "secret" place.

Conceivably one may be able to be alone, and yet the place may not be quiet. Such a circumstance will make a special demand on one's power of concentration. If you find that noises in the house or street distract you, stop your ears rather than lose your time. To derive the fullest benefit from the season of meditation you must close the doors of your mind to everything else.

Think about this for a moment or two before you read further, and *decide where you can find or fix up such a place.*

LET YOUR HEART BE STILL

The third requirement is *a right attitude of soul.*

Time and place will be of little avail if the spirit is wrong. There should be stillness within. If your soul is like a storm-tossed sea, if you are beaten about like a bird in a hurricane, if you rush into the divine presence like a horse into the battle, what hope is there of accomplishing anything in the short time at your disposal?

But, you may ask, should not the Quiet Time meet such a state as this, and produce in us the calm which we do not bring to it? Yes, certainly, if we definitely recognize our need, and go to him about it; but we shall have to be very definite. The majority of souls are hard pressed, and their experience can be expressed in the words of the hymn:

How oft in the conflict,
when press'd by the foe,
I have fled to my Refuge
and breathed out my woe;
How often when trials
like sea billows roll,
Have I hidden in Thee,
O Thou Rock of my soul.

The "secret place" is surely for such a troubled soul. But that soul's need calls for prayer rather than for Bible study; and in any case we must not allow ourselves to think that a distracted and tossed state of being represents normal Christian experience. Such a state is more akin to the hospital than to the battlefield. The Christian life does not consist in trying to keep our souls fit, but in being so fit that we are ready for the maximum accomplishment.

Assuming, therefore, a more or less normal condition, we should bring to the Quiet Time a spirit of stillness, or quickly secure it there. "Be still, and know that I am God." "In quietness and confidence shall be your strength."

EXPECT HIS PRESENCE

Expectancy is another necessity.

He who expects nothing will get nothing. It is the eager soul that will be made glad. If we will expose all our soul to the Holy Spirit, we shall have many a thrilling surprise.

I have already referred to the need of concentration but must stop to say that in the time chosen for our meditation, whether long or short, we must be *unhurried.* It is worse than useless to waste this precious time thinking about your next engagement. Be quiet. Concentrate. Expect. Don't hurry. Fifteen minutes of that will be much better than an hour of restless reading of the Word.

AIM ... AND ARRIVE

Fifth, *you must have an objective.*

If you aim at nothing, you are sure to hit it! Purpose should be behind all action; in all we do we should have an end in view.

Now, the object of the Quiet Time should not be to prepare addresses for your Bible study group, your Sunday school class or anything of the kind, but to nourish and upbuild your own soul. At such a time (I am talking of Bible meditation and not of prayer) it is not only right but necessary to forget others. For the idea of getting ready for a service draws your attention from your own personal need, and, in any case, the preparation of your own soul is the best preparation for every service. In the Quiet Time the consciousness of the soul must be,

"I need You, Oh, I need You."

Make perfectly clear to yourself each day as you begin your Quiet Time that you *cannot convey to others divine grace if you yourself have a neglected spiritual condition.* The object, therefore, of the Quiet Time should be self-examination and self-renewing. This personal element is prominent in the Psalms.

Ask yourself just here if your past disappointment has been due to your not having had an objective definite enough or, perhaps, having had a wrong objective.

HOW TO STUDY YOUR BIBLE

Now, having considered time, place, attitude, and objective, the next thing, and it is of supreme importance, is *a simple, practical and effective method.*

So many fail for want of this. To begin with, then, *plan your field of meditation.* You can do this on a small or great scale, but it should be done.

You may elect to meditate for a month upon some of the great texts of the Bible; or you may choose a Psalm—perhaps the 23rd—which you will devoutly contemplate without reference to the calendar; or you may select a number of great passages—such as John 17, 1 Corinthians 13, Hebrews 11—and work carefully through them; or you may prefer to take a book—such as John's Gospel, or Mark's or Ephesians, or 1 Peter—and *read these over and over again until like rain they saturate your thirsty soul.*

But about these suggestions I would say two things: First, if you plan on the big scale, you cannot take verse by verse, and word by word, as you would on the smaller scale, for that would too greatly protract the study, and variety is necessary for the maintenance of interest. But detailed consideration should be given to short chapters, to brief passages, and to verses.

Second, and this applies to any plan you may use, make your reading and study practical. Your objective in the Quiet Time is not so much to gather information as to gain inspiration, and so you should discover what is the application of what you read to your present circumstances and need. Turn the truth into terms of life, and use the Word to light and feed the fire of devotion.

Remember, you cannot lead anyone higher than you yourself have gone; you cannot enrich anyone beyond your own actual experience of God; hence the absolute necessity of the Bible in the Quiet Time.

Prayer in the Quiet Time

The cost of the daily prayer life is great. So great that unless we have a firm assurance that God has called us to spend this time with him each day, we shall never continue in the face of the prolonged initial difficulties, the subsequent occasional hindrances, and the sustained opposition of the enemy. If we are in earnest, we shall listen for God's call.

Christian biography abounds with illustrations of the fact that *the men who have moved the world for God have been men of sustained prayer habits*.

We must not model ourselves on the life of another—that way lies danger. God knows our lives, and he will not fail to direct as to when we are to meet with him, and for how long.

There is a tendency to think that we must acquire knowledge about praying before we begin to really pray. Have we here the explanation of the fact that while the demand for books on the subject of prayer is very large, praying Christians are comparatively few? Mr. Chadwick in *The Path of Prayer* writes, "Though a man shall have all knowledge about prayer, and though he understands all mysteries about prayer, unless he prays he will never learn to pray."

In this, as in other directions, ours is a life of faith. If God has made his purpose clear, we must step out in faith, and continue trustfully in the school of prayer.

THE COST OF PRAYER

It may help to mention the cost of faithfulness in prayer. I have in mind the keeping of the morning watch.

There is no assertion in the Bible that the morning watch is God's will for all, but there is not a little in typical incidents as well as in the utterances of the saints of God to suggest that the morning may be the normal time.

We move in a world which has no place for the prayer habit in its daily program. For other needs provision is made, but for prayer, none. In business life as well as at the university, the arrangement of the day leaves no room for quiet and undisturbed prayer. For this reason, as well as others, many arrive at the assurance that they are called to meet with God in a time captured from the morning hours of sleep.

The cost involved in doing this becomes apparent immediately.

Watchful discipline is needed in connection with the hour of retiring to rest, and such discipline is not only irksome but unpopular. Early rising is a new and uncomfortable habit which the body resists. Other sacrifices must be faced. The enemy will not fail to exaggerate difficulties. How many, in face of the cost, have stifled God's call and placed "impossible" as a barrier to an entry into the school of prayer.

Any later hour will have its cost—there will be no exemption. I quote again, *"The cost in the prayer life is not so much in the sweat of agonizing supplication as in the daily fidelity to the life of prayer. Nothing in the life of faith is so difficult to maintain."*

THE METHOD OF PRAYER

Praying is drawing near to God. It is opening our hearts to God. It is talking with him. Hebrews 10:19-22 freely and beautifully sets forth the basis and methods of drawing near to God.

This method is in two parts: God's provision and our responsibility. As always, God had to take this initiative to make prayer possible. And so in the person of his Son, our Savior Jesus Christ, we have access into the presence of God through the most precious blood of Christ. He is that new and living way. Through his broken body and shed blood he tore down the barrier separating God and man and made possible our entrance into the very throne-room of heaven. Christ is not only our sacrifice but our high priest. Through him we have the right to draw near to God.

But as believers we have a human responsibility. If we would draw near to God in prayer, we must draw near in sincerity—with a true heart. Deliberately, willingly, with a holy boldness and assurance of faith we approach the throne of grace. Reminding ourselves of Christ's sacrifice and priesthood for us, being assured of our position in him, recalling his invitation to come into God's presence, in sincerity we draw near.

In order to enter into the presence of God, our hearts must be cleansed. That first initial cleansing in the precious blood of Christ is not enough. For there is defilement through contact with sin after salvation, and this also must be cleansed.

When a Christian sins, his fellowship with God is broken. This does not mean that his life in Christ is lost, but he cannot commune with God. This fellowship can only be restored by a confession of sin. A confession that is as individual and specific as the sin itself. A confession that recognizes the sin in

God's sight and calls it by the name which God uses—lying, covetousness, jealousy, lack of love, impurity in word, thought and deed.

In drawing near to God in sincerity and faith we must make a complete confession of sin.

When we approach the Throne of Grace, our bodies must be washed with pure water—and that water is the Word of God. The most perfect preparation for a prayer period is the time spent before God in Bible reading, when by his Spirit and through his Word our hearts are searched, our bodies washed pure. So we may draw near.

All prayer should contain certain elements: There must be, first, confession. The realization that when we sin, we sin—in the final analysis—against God. Therefore, our sin must be confessed to him.

Then, surely, there must be the realization of the intense holiness and purity, the magnificent perfection, power and beauty of our God. We do well to be quiet in his presence, to think of him as Isaiah saw him in the temple, high and lifted up; as John saw him at Patmos, when he fell at his feet as dead.

Then, should we not praise him, when we remember with gratitude and thanksgiving the great things that God has done for us, for which we are glad? Should we not bless the

Lord with all our souls as we remember his benefits, spiritual and material?

After confession, worship and adoration, praise and thanksgiving, will come a time of intercession—a time when we bear up before the Lord those persons and activities which he has laid upon our hearts, when we plead for representatives on the foreign field, when we enter into the heart of God, thinking his thoughts after him.

And last of all, we think of ourselves. We will present ourselves before the Lord that he may lay his hand upon us in blessing, that we may more and more be conformed to the image of his Son, that Christ may be magnified in our mortal bodies, and that he may be formed in us. Petitions for ourselves will always come last.

Then as we pray, we pray in the name of the Lord Jesus, not using this phrase as an empty shibboleth, but being conscious of him and all that his name means.

Praying is working. Intense and prolonged prayer is physically and mentally exhausting. We must bear in mind our motive. If, as we pray, our motive is that *we* might be blessed, that *we* might be used, that the glory of *our* name or of *our* organization might be magnified; if we seek power with God and power with men for ourselves—then we do not pray according to his will and we do not have our requests.

But, if we are enabled—in a sense—to forget ourselves and to pray for one purpose and to one end only, the joy and satisfaction and the glory of our Savior—then we shall really begin to pray effectively and according to God's will. Only God himself can bring us to that glorious position and condition "where that earthly part of me glows with that power divine." May he teach us to always remember that our "goal is God himself, not joy nor peace nor even blessings, but himself, our God."

SOME PRACTICAL SUGGESTIONS FOR THE QUIET TIME

The Quiet Time is not just a spiritual exercise with no down-to-earth dimensions. Here are some suggestions for solving some very practical problems.

ON WAKING UP

Go to bed in time! Late nights are the relentless enemy of the Quiet Time. It is physically impossible habitually to sit up to the small hours of the morning watching television or talking with one's friends and then to get up each morning fit for a proper Quiet Time.

The Devil will fight a man here. He must be fought back. Here lies the initial victory. Pray the night before about your getting up.

As for getting up, Dr. Holden used to stress the fact that all that is required is a "momentary act of the will." Once the bedclothes are off it is scarcely worth going back to bed again. The battle is lost or won during the few seconds which elapse between waking and a purposeful movement of hand or foot.

Get wide awake before starting your reading or prayer. It is probably better to complete ablutions of all kinds and to dress fully before any part of the Quiet Time is attempted. Some find it even better to go for a short jog or to do setting-up exercises.

If you tend to get drowsy, change your position at once. While kneeling is obviously the most befitting position for a person to adopt when approaching the divine Father, if you persistently find that kneeling induces sleep, it would seem better reverently to take some other posture. "The late Bishop of Durham used to read the Word and to pray standing or walking in the grounds of Auckland Castle." It may be well to add, however, that on no account must these considerations be made an excuse for laziness, and standing is to be preferred to any unnecessarily lax position.

When reading the Scriptures, it is best regularly to sit in the same position at a comfortable desk. Distracting, gaudy-covered books should be removed and everything planned for comfort and the greatest possible concentration.

THE RIGHT APPROACH

Let your first conscious thoughts on waking be of your Savior whom you are rising to meet. He is waiting for you. *He has been interceding for you through the night watches.*

At the commencement, a moment or two of quiet thought in which you are reminded of the aim of the Quiet Time is essential if you are really to appreciate the presence of God.

Bring back your thoughts again and again during your reading and prayer to the fact that you are not alone. Two of you are sharing the room and the Bible. Reverently remind yourself of his presence by your side. *He is there.* The realization of this fact makes the Quiet Time a living reality.

Don't do all the talking!

There should be stillness and expectancy (Ps. 46:10). "God reveals himself to you, not as you struggle to get into his presence and to 'feel' him, but as you yield freely to him." This does not mean that you are to make your mind a blank—but that the attitude of reception is necessary as you concentrate your thoughts on the glorious person of Christ and meditate on the Scriptures you have read, thinking into their inner meaning.

The Holy Spirit reveals the deeper things only to those who are at leisure to receive from him the secrets of the Scriptures.

Whether the time available is long or short, it must be unhurried (Is. 30:15). If there is not much time available, do not attempt to crowd in too much.

Come to the Bible and prayer willing to obey and to put into practice all he shows you, instantaneously and unquestioningly (Jn. 8:31-32).

USING TIME TO THE BEST ADVANTAGE

If possible, commence your Quiet Time at the same hour each morning. This practice will make it easier both to be regular in your meeting with God and also to gain adequate time.

You may ask, "How long shall I devote to my Quiet Time? What is the minimum?"

No rule can be given. The details of each individual's university, business, or home associations differ. The most that can be said is that those whose lives have been fruitful in Christ's service have tended to take every opportunity of lengthening the times of their communion with God. Spiritual maturity will demand a longer time than that which a new convert may find difficult to fill.

A minimum of twenty minutes has been suggested by some; others would set this limit for Bible reading alone. God knows all the limitations or advantages of your circumstances, and it is really a question of what is the maximum I can gain to give him.

The ideal is to have more time than "enough" at your disposal. Try to err on the liberal side, just as you like to do when you meet another you love. You must, if possible, have time enough to forget time. But, in any case, aim at quality rather than quantity.

When you have decided how long you will spend, aim at some definite but simple plan. But do not be rigidly tied to it. If your usual practice is 50% Bible reading and 50% prayer, be prepared for God to lead you from time to time to change that proportion. Be flexible. Avoid "ruts."

As regards the order of Bible study and prayer, it may be of interest to add that George Müller always read his Bible first and then prayed, because he always found something new for which to praise God as he read the Scriptures. He found that proceeding in this order made his prayers living and fresh each day.

It may be that some Christians who find themselves praying in almost the same phrases each day would be well advised to feed their prayers in this manner, for example, praising God for what they have just read of his attributes and asking him for those things which they have just discovered that they lack. But, of course, commence with a brief prayer for new light to be given from the Scriptures.

BIBLE STUDY METHODS

Some method is necessary as to the order of reading the Scriptures. There are several methods of reading through the Bible in one, two or three years according to the time which is available each day. For the Quiet Time the Scriptures must be approached mainly from the devotional standpoint.

A *notebook should be used* in which to write thoughts which the Holy Spirit may give you as you read and peruse your morning's portion. But do not attempt too elaborate note-taking, as this will tend to distract your attention.

Remember that you are coming to the Scriptures at these times for the satisfaction of your own needs. Reading in order to help others, or to prepare addresses, should normally be done at other times.

If you are not getting much from your daily reading, cross-examine yourself:

Is there any *example* for me to follow?

Is there any *command* for me to obey?

Is there any *error* for me to avoid?

Is there any *sin* for me to forsake?

Is there any *promise* for me to claim?

Is there any *new thought about God Himself?*

PRAYER

Remember that prayer does not mean a mere recital of things which you need. Daily prayer should contain at least some of the following: thanksgiving (see the Psalms); worship (consider the names of God); confession (see 1 Jn.); intercession for others (Rom. 15:30); and committal of the new day to Christ.

It is doubtful if any Christian should let a day pass without having devoutly thanked the Lord Jesus for Calvary.

There are methods for regularly remembering certain needs daily, and others at weekly or monthly intervals. But beware of any method which is too complicated.

Avoid formality. As soon as prayer becomes formal, it is really dead. Ask God to show you what is wrong. Has sin, or a careless, lazy spirit come between him and you? Remember the hint which seems to be enshrined in George Müller's method, as indicated above.

Some Christians find it easier to spend a longer period in the morning and to devote their shorter evening period chiefly to prayer. Others who have to leave early by train each morning have been able to compensate a shortened morning Quiet Time by a longer one at night.

Many Christians misuse their Sundays. Make the best use of the extra free time, and do not fall into the trap of shortening your Quiet Time because you are going to spend the greater part of the day in Christian worship and service. *That* is what the day is for!

IF YOU MISS A MORNING

If you miss your Quiet Time for one reason or another, do not imagine that the day will necessarily be a failure. It need not be. If the fault is yours, confess it, obtain immediate cleansing, and as you go out into the day claim the full power of the Holy Spirit for that day. If the fault is not yours, remember that God on his side is not necessarily limited by the amount of time his servant has spent in direct communion with him. He is sovereign.

Do not regard the Quiet Time as having a mechanical connection with divine blessing. It is our highest wisdom to spend as much time with God as we are able, but he does not use us merely because we have spent so much time in prayer or preparation.

If you have no sense of his presence and feel that your prayer is empty and worthless, tell him about it quite frankly. At the same time tell him that you believe he is there because of his promises (Jn. 14:16; Heb. 13:5; Mt. 28:20), and that you know he will answer prayer quite independently of your feelings.

THE PROBLEM OF CONCENTRATION

Finally, there are some Christians who find it very difficult to concentrate. There is a great need of perseverance in avoiding wandering thoughts. The apostle meant this when he wrote to the Ephesians of the need to "keep alert with all perseverance" (Eph. 6:18).

The secret lies in the person of our Lord. Though there may be many who find it difficult to concentrate their thoughts on abstractions, few are unable to think about a person whom they really love! But they may argue that they have seen those they love on earth and that the person of our Lord seems to them little more than an abstraction. It is precisely for these people that the Quiet Time is absolutely indispensable!

Nothing could be of greater importance than that no Christian when praying should be under any illusion concerning the reality of Christ's person. The Bible—particularly the New Testament—definitely teaches us that faith is not a vague, intangible, subjective influence. It is presented as an instrument by which the individual Christian is enabled to grasp the unseen and to come into the enjoyment of God's provision for him. In the case of the person of Christ, the New Testament leads us to believe that by faith we are able to see him in a manner which (though it differs in kind) may be as real as physical sight. To those who have seen Christ (in the Gospel sense) there is no unreality about the vision.

The reason for the difficulty appears to lie in the fact that the greater part of Christendom is occupied with the principles, ethics and ideals of the faith, rather than with the person who embodies them all.

The greatest need for us all is to become more Christo-centric in our thinking. The very people who complain of their inability to concentrate on the person of Christ are to be seen using photos to remind themselves of absent loved ones, whom they assert are real to them. Why, then, do they not make more use of the full portrait of Christ enshrined in the sacred Scriptures? No true seeker who has ever read through the Gospels, earnestly desiring the Holy Spirit's aid, has failed to see the moral beauty of Christ and a true likeness of his person. Let us carry the impressions of that likeness with us as we go to prayer. Those who find it difficult to do so should saturate their minds with all they can in the Gospels and the Epistles.

What special viewpoints of our Lord's many-sided character do we need chiefly to carry with us to prayer?

All Bible teachers would probably agree that after the cross (which must ever be kept before us), we should do well to concentrate more on the resurrection and the throne.

How many Christians really live in the daily enjoyment of our Lord's present position of authority at the right hand of God's throne?

We would urge those who have difficulty in concentrating, first to allow the scriptural portrait of the cross to come before them, and then to turn their thoughts to the glorified Christ in whom all power now resides. The books of Hebrews and Revelation give these portraits.

When the Christian church awakes to the true glory of her Lord's presence, and really grasps the reality of his resurrection power, in that day there will be a mighty revival. God is willing. Are you?

THE PERSONAL PASSION FOR CHRIST

There is a passion for Christ which has been given to very few to possess, but which has set those who have it apart for ever from their fellow men.

Is not this the quality which separates between Christian and Christian, which marks out some—the rare ones—as being apart from the rest of us?

Is it not this quality in the writing of the mystics which, as in no other spiritual literature, pulls at our heart strings and creates a pain of longing?

Those marvellous "friends of God" had the personal passion for Christ.

Samuel Rutherford had it too, and in his bleak prison he could write, "One smile of Christ's face is now to me as a kingdom."

The trouble with the rest of us is that we are content to dwell in Jerusalem without seeing the face of the King. We are hard at work for him; the freighted hours rush by leaving us scarcely time to give a thought to the Lover of our souls who is longing for our friendship.

And when we do go into the audience chamber, we are burdened with requests—business that must be put through, guidance we need here, help there, petitions on behalf of this one or that.

All important, all urgent, all worthy, but—just business.

Amidst the terrific onrush of the apostasy, amidst the swirl of pleasure which is engulfing the majority of those who call themselves Christians, God has his own, his seven thousand, "all the knees which have not bowed to Baal, and every mouth which has not kissed him."

They are men and women whose faith and zeal burn brighter as the world's darkness deepens. They are ready to die at Jerusalem, or anywhere, for their Lord. They are valiant for the truth, and wield the sword lustily on God's behalf. Nevertheless, few have that passion for Christ which Paul expressed in the words, "To me to live is Christ."

There is so much splendid orthodoxy that leaves people cold, so much preaching of "the simple gospel" that excites no enthusiasm. People can sit and listen to the story of Calvary with dry eyes and no quickened heartbeat. *In the telling of that story there is no ring of personal passion for the One from whose "head, and hands, and feet, sorrow and love flow mingled down."*

But now and again—at rare intervals—one meets someone who, like Paul, has looked into the matchless face of Jesus, and who henceforth sees nothing save the face of his Beloved.

There is a radiance about such a one, a glory shining forth, a wonderful quality of voice and handclasp, a fragrance unmistakable. "The smell of their garments is as the smell of Lebanon with all chief spices." These keep company with their Beloved in the place where there are a "fountain of gardens, a well of living waters and streams from Lebanon."

What makes the difference?

It is *not* knowledge, for knowledge puffs up. We have knowledge in abundance nowadays. God has given us great teachers of his Word. Many of us have reached the place where we think we are competent to pass judgment upon others, and where we say, though not as the Psalmist said it, "I have more understanding than all my teachers." But too often our knowledge is a form of godliness, the power of which we are denying because we do not possess it.

No, it is not knowledge that makes the difference, nor is it orthodoxy, nor zeal, nor works.

What was it that made Moses the lawgiver, the interpreter of Sinai's thunder, as keenly appreciative of the grace of God as was even

Paul himself? Just this: Moses was the incomparable "friend of God" because he possessed a passion for God in an unusual degree. That passion had consumed every last vestige of personal ambition, so that when God offered him something that might legitimately have tempted him, especially as coming from the source it did, it made no difference to the man to whom God's good name meant more than all besides.

Is there anything so sublime anywhere in sacred story as Moses' refusal to go on without God, as recorded in Exodus 33? As a concession to his pleading on behalf of the people who had so deeply sinned against God, an angel had been promised to guide them in the way. The Lord had said to Moses, "Depart, go up hence ... I will send an angel before you ... I will not go up among you, lest I consume you in the way."

But Moses had long companied with God, and it was unthinkable that now the wondrous Presence should be withdrawn. An angel might be all right for other people, but not for the man who was accustomed to talking with God "face to face, as a man speaks to his friends."

And so in a marvellous argumentation Moses put the matter before the Lord, carrying his point step by step until he reached the place where he dared to say no to God. "If your presence doesn't go with me, don't carry us up hence."

In the grief of that sad day, how glad God must have been to find one man who at all costs wanted the best, and how gladly he must have said to Moses, "This very thing that you have spoken I will do ... My presence will go with you, and I will give you rest."

God never forgot it. The time came when that friend failed him; nevertheless at the end they went both together up the slopes of Nebo's lonely mountain, communing as they walked, and there God gave his beloved friend sleep, and with his own hands laid him away to rest until the great resurrection day. God did not consider angelic ministration good enough that day for the man who in his lifetime would have nothing less than God himself.

David also possessed in a marked degree that passion for God. His flesh and his heart cried out for the living God. His psalms reveal this passion ever throbbing in his soul. Only in the light of that passion can the imprecatory psalms be rightly understood. David hated with a perfect hatred them that hate God, and counted them his enemies. Sin to him—his own or others'—held its deepest stain and its sharpest sting because it was done "against you and you only." When we possess this passion for God that David had, we too shall know "the exceeding sinfulness of sin."

In the New Testament, Paul is the outstanding example of the man who is dominated by the passion for Christ, as apart from his devotion to the cause of Christ. That passion was surely born in those three days in which he was beholding "the glory of God in the face of Jesus Christ"—sightless days, but filled with radiance.

Paul might easily have become hard and critical and bitter in the stress of controversial conflict. The passion for the person of Christ, as apart from loyalty to his cause, kept him from that. And so, speaking after the manner of men, we see him fighting the beasts at Ephesus, and yet homesick to "depart and be with Christ, which is far better."

The great tender heart of love in Paul that made him the nursing father of the infant churches had its fountainhead in his all-absorbing personal passion for Christ, to know the love of whom—its breadth, and length, and depth and height—is to be "filled with all the fulness of God."

There were others also.

Two humble women were admitted into that inner-most circle. Mary of Bethany and the Magdalene knew something of that priceless relationship with our Lord. It was Mary's devotion to the person of Christ that led her instinctively and unerringly to do the thing that pleased him by annointing his feet. In contrast to her love is the cold orthodoxy of the disciples who would have been satisfied if the ointment had been sold for three hundred pence and given to the poor. Almsgiving, according to the Pharisees, was the chief element in righteousness. But there would always be time for that. "The poor you have always with you," said Jesus, and his heart was comforted by the love of Mary, fragrant as her poured-out ointment. What a privilege was hers to comfort him in the days when "his soul began to be sorrowful, even unto death!"

It was that same passion for Christ which held Mary Magdalene weeping by the empty tomb when the disciples had gone away again to their own homes. And how wondrously she was rewarded! Not only vision of angels but Christ himself to gladden her heart and dry her tears; and it is written for ever that "he appeared *first* to Mary Magdalene."

In our zeal for the better are we missing the best?

The word of our Lord to us is still, "He who loves me will be loved by my Father, and I will love him and manifest myself to him." Up there, "his servants shall serve him, and they shall see his face," but it is also blessedly true that he will manifest himself on earth to those who love and serve him here.

There is reward for the obedient disciples,

there is power and authority for the faithful disciples, there is glory of achievement for the zealous disciples ... but there is the whisper of God's love, there is the joy of his presence, and the shining of his face for those who love him for himself alone. And "to what profit is it that we dwell in Jerusalem, if we do not see the face of the King?"